To Julie

ICED

with love

x

ALSO BY ALISON CHISHOLM

ICED

Poems in celebration of a Diamond Birthday

Alison Chisholm

First published in 2012
by Caleta Publishing

Cover photograph by Malcolm Chisholm

ISBN 978-1-4717-4741-0

Printed and bound by Lulu.com

ACKNOWLEDGEMENTS

Some of these poems have appeared in *Acumen, Orbis, Common Threads, Writing Magazine, Awesome!* or have been broadcast by *BBC Radio Merseyside.* Others have won awards in the Sefton Poetry Competition, Accent on Poetry Competition, *Orbis* Readers' Award, Elizabeth Longford Poetry Competition, and various contests in the NFSPS and Ohio Poetry Day Competitions.

DREDGING DIAMONDS

I remember sitting under the table,
leaves collapsed to form a rigid cat's-cradle around me
smelling of wood and lavender wax,
of dinners and teas, don't talk with your mouth full,
elbows off. Andy Pandy, Looby Loo and Teddy
have the hamper's wicker lid closed on their heads.
I cry. Mum makes her only complaint to the BBC.

I'm holding Mummy's hand in big school,
and Jill's there holding her Mummy's hand,
and we're big girls now so we don't cry.
Just two weeks later we move house,
and I have to find a way to fill new spaces
in rooms that echo the wrong sounds,
in a classroom where everyone else has a best friend.

A tiny pink girl
snuffles and snuggles, makes us
a whole family.

Beyond the Biggest Spotty Dog in the World
I find the oldest music teacher in the world,
learn scales and songs until Beethoven rolls over
to make room for the Beatles, Monkees, the Beach Boys;
and boys.

We move
again, and I,
wrenched from school, youth club, friends,
become the teenaged monster, vile
wild child.

Dad conjures a respite ,
rings the local theatre, introduces me;
I pause mid-protest to audition.
I'm watching as the set collapses,
exposes shamefaced stagehands; look at one
      and
Romeo and Juliet
   Antony and Cleopatra
      Albert and Victoria
         Tristan and Isolde
            Napoleon and Josephine
are downgraded to passing fancies.
This is Love.

The sky never looked
like this before, gunmetal
grey, hot, holding time
while the *I do* promises
ricochet around the stars.

I am spattered head to foot with peach emulsion.
Our three year old daughter stays with Nana and Grandad
when I rush to the hospital.
Her baby sister arrives - prompt, quick, tidy, efficient -
setting the future pattern.

There follows a chaos of trips to the park,
treks through Pompei, batches of scones baked and shared,
Sunday roasts and a game of cards, choosing a kitten,
feeding squirrels, letters to Santa, swimming the pool's length.
Passing parcels and musical chairs
count years and minutes, merge and bed themselves deep
in the morass of time as it spirals ever faster.

But no weight
of ordinary days
dims the diamonds.

57%

More than half of me is water
trapped in bone and muscle,
pumped through arteries, turned to saliva,
bile and sweat. This water knows
no trilling over stream-bed's pebbles
seeking rivers, dancing out to sea;
no pull of breeze to vaporise in clouds,
free-fall and drench parched gardens.
Instead it keeps my skin from desiccating,
brain from atrophying, heart and liver
from being ground to dust.

I open a bottle. Uncapped, it bubbles over.
I feel water fizz on my tongue,
sense its elation to escape
constraint of glass. It slips down my gullet,
settles, complacent, in my stomach -
does not know consummation will make it
my better half.

UNDERFOOT

No compromise for Pharaohs. Only gold
was rich enough embellishment to blaze
on jewellery, clothing, shoes. Now sterile, cold,
great Tutankhamen's chattels still amaze

in rich enough embellishment. To blaze
his message, craftsmen laboured hour on hour -
(great Tutankhamen's chattels still amaze) -
made gem-starred chests and thrones to prove his power.

His message: craftsmen laboured hour on hour
to show how standing still is mere defeat;
made gem-starred chests and thrones to prove his power,
and fixed his enemies beneath his feet.

To show how standing still is mere defeat
they made his sandals icons, took gold thread
and fixed his enemies beneath his feet
by drawing them where sole and heel would tread.

They made his sandals icons; took gold thread,
stitched images of foes that he could quell
by drawing them where sole and heel would tread,
(humiliation worse for them than hell.)

Stitched images of foes that he could quell
were crushed by time, each victory turned to dross -
humiliation worse for them than hell -
when mighty kingdoms crumbled into dust.

Where crushed by time, each victory turned to dross
on jewellery, clothing, shoes - now sterile, cold.
When mighty kingdoms crumbled into dust,
no compromise: for Pharaohs, only gold.

TIME BOMB

I tread straight paths, right angles -
don't cut corners and churn up grass -
I pay my bills, drive inside speed limits,
sort rubbish for recycling. I am there
if a neighbour needs help, try to practise
what is preached at me, clean up
if my dog fouls the park. My voice
is still and small, to calm
when politicians rant, when children bicker;

but inside I am roaring, yelling,
swearing to the heavens, while my rage
is magma throbbing to erupt. I am
the instant Banner becomes The Hulk,
finger on the psychopath's trigger,
moment between button and missile.

I know the right course. I brush my teeth,
comb my hair, walk neatly to church
….. ticking ….. ticking ….. ticking …..

MUSEE DES BEAUX-ARTS, NANTES

Marooned in the centre of the square hall
a narrow white gondola is beached,
pointed prow and stern angled to corners.
No taller than my knee, she bisects
the space, slices air heavied with awe.
Her slightness is illusion, for she bears
a cargo of nine planets, each smoothed,
unblemished, waiting to be launched.

I would touch, but something more
than protocol prevents me. Instead
I stand at time's dawn,
part of a petrified moment,
hold my breath until a greater power
spills the cargo, sends it spinning
to find its sun.

Yet even as I watch, I know
the paradox, that neither I nor installation
would be here if that outpouring
of Mercury, Saturn, Pluto had not happened.

I am rooted, on the cusp between
the planets' birthing and their hurtle
into greater darkness of the sun's demise.
The gallery recedes, paintings pale and blur
to nothingness, height and breadth and length
have no significance.

A voice across the void calls my name,
asks if I noticed this or that,
wonders if I want coffee. I am pulled
into the trivia of day, force my feet

to walk towards the exit, resist
an urge to look back. For now
there is no need to look. I know a future past
where everything is changed.

UNSPOKEN

'No needs for words'
he used to say, believing
she knew exactly how he felt.
He told her cards
were empty-headed, trite
pieces of nonsense,
a waste of time and cash,
tomorrow's garbage.
He made a joke
of never buying her a birthday gift;
said it would only serve to remind
that she was growing older.
Besides, he prided himself
on generosity in housekeeping,
didn't mind when she bought
a dress, new shoes.
He cared for her,
worked hard - good pay, good pension -
never raised a hand to her,
would cook and clean if she was ill.
But oh, how much she longed
for the gift he never gave:
to hear him say he loved her.

NOT MY FAULT

It isn't quick, it isn't painless
when someone hacks your head off,
chopping through flesh and fat,
bone and sinew with an axe. You feel
each blow resonating in your limbs,
know blood's spurt in your fur.

And I am not to blame; it is my nature
to eat when food appears, use wiles
to get my way. If anyone's at fault
it's a mother who lets her idiot child
skip through my forest in blaring red,
her basket stuffed with pies and cake.

I approached her, asked her first,
and she refused to share. So who's surprised
I ran ahead and hid and waited?
The nightgown? That was a coup,
although in truth I didn't really look
like Granny. Her mistake
shows once again the girl's stupidity.

I'd have been happy with a piece of pie
but hunger overtook, and she looked
so succulent with those plump little arms,
delicious round belly.

She started that inane conversation -
big ears, big eyes, big teeth. Did no-one tell her
how rude it is to make personal remarks?

My mouth was watering by then.
I knew how tasty she'd be,

could not stop my jaws from slavering.
Then there he stood, axe menacing,
eyes filled with hate. And here I am,

feeling pain subside at last
as rigor sets in, and the forest's scavengers
are moving closer to peck my eyes,
worm through my coat, leave maggot eggs
to fatten on dead flesh. It's not my fault.
It's not.
Not.

SEA SORCERY

Bewitched by spindrift, I explore the sand,
my fingers inching grain by silvered grain
where froth of wave skims, skitters to the land.
Above the sound of sea, I hear a strain
of mermaid song, a high and plaintive call
answered by seagulls wheeling through the sky.
I squeeze a knot of bladderwrack, inhale
its salted, oily scent. A whispered sigh
of breeze through marram grass along the beach
soothes troubled thoughts. I start to feel new hope
empower me, and convince me I can reach
a state of peace; I grasp and clutch the rope.
    Sea's sorcery, in driftwood, stone and shell,
    works magic mortal logic can't dispel.

O CAPTAIN! MY CAPTAIN!

I see her leaning on the desk,
see the nylon jumper, tweed pencil skirt,
almost-sensible shoes. She never
had to raise her voice -
one gimlet glance said all.

I held my breath as, term by term,
she cast us, and I thrilled
to Helena, Miranda, Rosalind,
wrung my hands as Lady Macbeth,
wielded daggers over Caesar.

When she recited, poems came to life.
My skates hissed to Wordsworth's *Prelude*,
I learned the weight
of an albatross around my neck,
choked before I fitted Owen's gas mask.

I strained to read her cramped hieroglyphs,
longing to discover praise
for laboured homework; scoring once
when I had to ask her to interpret
spider scribbles. They said *illegible*.

She was our hero, nearly our friend
in days when teachers were remote.
I never wavered in my worship of her,
even when I was banned from Eng. Lit.
for fear of holding back the class.

I've only met her once since then.
Chance brought us to adjacent handbasins
in town's most stylish powder room.

I longed to remind her who I was, tell her
how she'd helped me to become a poet.

I caught that glance in the mirror,
heard in my head my thirteen-year voice chant
Good Morning, Miss O'Donoghue -
and couldn't speak. I passed her a paper towel.
Our hands didn't touch.

UNDER GROUND

We are unsung heroes,
we tiny worms of white,
forcing our way unseen, unnoticed.

We are frail,
vulnerable when spade intrudes -
determined enough to edge among crumbs of soil,
find our toehold.

We are the anchors
that secure breeze blown stems,
channels for water, nutrients,
umbilical filaments.

You may admire
first green spike, slender shaft,
bud, blossom and bloom;
but never forget
our silent chambers,
our grip under ground.

ANOTHER BOAT, ANOTHER RIVER

Picture a boy, blitz-born, aunt-nurtured,
coaxed to the seaside by seafaring father.
Can you feel the wrench of choice:
Me or your mother? New Zealand or Woolton?

See cellophane flowers in the *Mendips* garden,
regulated lawn and bushes, Sunday school,
tidy house, tidy living. Who could resist
the challenge to climb trees in Strawberry Fields?

At the morning room table, sun in your eyes,
let your hand - as his - skim the promise
of blank paper, fill it with sketches,
jokes, cartoons, images of Alice, Mr. Toad.

Do you know the frustration of being different -
the need to fight your way through school
armed with dirty jokes and ready fists,
tormenting teachers, your head in the clouds?

Imagine you are just an apronstring away
from wrong-side-of-the-track culture; cultured
to fit in, determined not to conform,
your mother's son, plasticine Elvis clone.

Reach for a guitar. Pluck. Strum. Find, like him,
discordant crash that sets the whole world rocking.
The looking glass of your life splinters.
Kaleidoscope-drenched diamonds fill your sky.

WRITERS' CONFERENCE: THE LAST NIGHT

It's Thursday, and we've talked all week
of poetry and novels. Tonight
there is nothing to do but listen
while men in flannels, blazers, old valley ties
sing. We sit in murmuring rows
in a stark grey lecture hall. This choir
is unpronounceably Welsh, overstuffed
with consonants. The conductor is hailed,
baton tapped; there's a second's pause
      and
           then
the very air trembles beneath
weight of eighty voices, six parts
in harmony so absolute it shames the angels.
These are the voices of lambing in midwinter,
of the pithead's labour and loss,
of rugby finals and Chapel on Sunday.
These are the voices of minstrel and bard,
descendants of Llewellyn and Merlin.

We sway to spirituals, hum along with traditional airs,
man *Les Miserables* barricades,
thrill to the music of the Phantom's night,
weep to survey the wondrous cross:
      and
          finally
when all stand at the first chords
of *Mae Hen Wlad Fy Nhadau*
and none of us can recognise a word,
we gape at sheer beauty
of that glory of voices
singing for our pleasure, singing for love,
singing the soul of Wales.

THONG SONG

When you're twenty, maybe twenty-two
and lying on the beach
with a stomach like an ironing board
and bottom like a peach
all tanned and bronzed and glowing,
it's acceptable - well just -
to split the orbs with stringy thongs
(that's if you really must.)
But beware that if you stand and walk
or paddle in the sea
you'll chafe, and itch in places
where to scratch lacks dignity.

However ...

when you're twenty stone or twenty-two
and lying on the shore
with a bellyfull of stretchmarks
and a butt that's rather more
like a pair of watermelons
full of dimpled cellulite
than a peach - you should remember
that it really isn't right
to divide the mass of blubber
with garottes like razor wire,
leaving twin blancmanges wobbling
while the thong is riding higher.
When the time comes to remove it
the extraction is extreme,
and you hate to have to touch it
as you know just where it's been.
So when you shop for swimwear

buy some shorts, eschew the thong;
for both stylishness and comfort
it is absolutely wrong.

FLIGHT HAIKUS

The hover moment
stalls; pause; smooth ascent begins,
air-kisses goose skein.

Crystals of sky ice
freckle windows, frame billows
where clouds rock like waves.

Your hand is my rock.
I clutch it when turbulence
threatens my still life.

Trapped in my skin, half
amazed, half fearful, I float;
whisper 'Hello, God.'

PLAYING THE GAME

To leave school is to know
you will never again have to don
modesty's divided skirt, an aertex shirt,
and pound the quarter mile of path round classrooms
facing sniggers from smug students
warm-basking in French or physics.
You will never again have to freeze at full back
or risk shins beneath a hail of hockey sticks
where bullying is encouraged.

You will never again catch the school bus,
be trundled off to the town pool;
yelled at to speed up your front crawl, back crawl,
breast and butterfly; warned
you'll walk three miles back unless you hurry,
made to drag clothes on your still-damp body,
swimsuit squelching in your schoolbag.

You will never again be forced
to heave your weight up ropes,
leap the vaulting horse that bruised your thighs,
skip until a stitch makes you sick.

Never will you be branded *goal attack*
or *wing defence*, never wield a raquet
at tennis ball or shuttlecock, never race
your adolescent nakedness through showers
with thirty others.

And whatever life throws at you in the future,
you can rest assured the nobody
will ever make you play the game again.

BETRAYED

First glimpse across a crowded shop
quickened my heart, trembled knees
with lust and love. I had to have them,
to possess the brilliant yellow court shoes,
heels that raised my feet near vertical,
toes tapering to gleaming arrows,
soles that glared defiance
through the *Less Than Half Price*
blazoned on their label.
I caressed the box,
hugged it all the way home.

My love was unrequited.

Buttery leather turned vice
to grip my toes and squeeze and squeeze,
to chafe and redden heels. Arches ached
from backward bending, and only lunge and grab
foiled the conspiracy between stiletto and stair carpet,
saved me from tumbling.

I kept them in the wardrobe for a while,
hoped to tame them
by coaxing with shoe-stretchers,
breaking them in with five-minute forays.
They refused to be broken,
took to lurking in corners,
brash, malevolent.

Today they strut the charity store window,
gleam and preen, luring passers-by;
while I, seduced, rejected,
turn my gaze to trainers, sandals, brogues.

DROWNED

Water is new to me. In cave's dry dust
I learned only liquid of ink he made
by crushing berries. Now I feel
an overwhelming salted wetness flood my pages,
drenching words.

Through all these years I have been
his friend, his solace, closer
than a lover. I watched
as shock of betrayal was replaced
by resignation, heard him thank empty air
for his courtier's gift of books.

While he observed and read and studied,
I waited to receive
the distillation of his knowledge,
conspired with him to record
how to whip storms into being
then stay the ocean, how
to conjure music from silence.

I knew his secret
for freeing airy spirits trapped in trees,
shared his delight to see a child turn woman,
sensed his rage
when the beast assaulted her.

Summoning this tempest was his masterstroke.
I knew from notes - still small and neat
despite his speed in writing - that he meant
to challenge those who'd wronged him,
gain the means to leave our island;
finding a prince deserving of his daughter

was a bonus he could not have guessed.

I never thought that he'd abandon me,
still less he'd drown me, plummet deeped.
But now I sense myself disintegrate, and feel
our words dissolved to traces smeared
on pearl and coral
forgotten fathoms down.

STITCHING POPPIES

My needle brings trees to bud,
shifts light clouds through the sky,
ripens a field of grain,
and then the poppies start. I cross-stitch
rank on rank of them; shade them bright red,
scarlet, deep crimson, with salmon pink echoes,
black hearts at the centre.

They flaunt their presence, flirt with corn stalks,
make play of breeze in brazen dance, twirl
harlot skirts beneath the weight of heat,
heady with their promise - charmed sleep.

Only when the coil of silk
is stilled, when glass
fixes flower images, do I see
stemmed blood that blots a foreign field,
November's starkest message,
and rows too numerous to count
of balsa crosses gashed with poppy heads.

THE WAY THE COOKIE CRUMBLES

It might have been a heart attack
while I sat in twilight
watching *Aida* with real elephants.
It might have been a plane
nosediving into the Atlantic
on engine-failed prayers;
or cyanide turning me blue
while my lover's wife looked on.
It might have been an Isadora moment,
a Monroe drama,
disaster-movie inferno.

But no. Here I am at the bus stop
feeling life ebb out of me
as an out-of-control bin lorry
mounts the pavement and keeps coming.

And I have wasted
so many last-thought moments
on preferable endings,
there isn't even time
for my life to flash befo ....

LITTERMATES

Byron and Shelley sit before the fire,
their long tails touching,
siblings who need to feel each other near.

In sleep they share one basket,
cuddle close, paws around necks,
purring their delight.

Washing is a harsh-tongued caress,
or random licks at ears and shoulders,
preening between each other's delicate toes.

Fearless in dangerous sports,
they leap from chair to sofa,
make our living room an obstacle course.

Outdoors, twin tigers stalk
butterfly and beetle,
wiggle and pounce on fallen leaves.

But nestled together in my arms,
a perfect couplet of ginger and tabby,
Byron and Shelley become a poem.

'AMETHYST SPRAY'

They were the last flowers he gave her, a supermarket posy
affectedly named, an afterthought in purple, wine and white.
Not just a gift, not quite apology,
they bristled in cut glass,
the table's focus, grimly clenched to prove
the boast that they'd be good for seven days.

He'd gone before they dropped,
a mess of blood and bone, impacted steering wheel,
glass splinters fixing shock to frozen eyes and mouth.

Every vase and jug she had was crammed
with pastel, heavy-scented evidence
of eye-blink's life change, sympathy, empathy;
of ritual, perfect and brittle as the petals
stiffening on his dusky flowers. Hand-tied bouquets
smirked while, hopelessly, she tried
to lift a gerbera's limp head, or stripped
crisped leaves from a chrysanthemum's stem.

Afterwards she shook their lounge -
her living room - into cushion-plumped normality;
recycled cards, composted half dead flowers. Only
his remained, fetid water choking her breath,
asparagus fern dust blurring the polish.

She changed the water, watched
decay's relentless crawl until his gift
tainted her space with death's obscenity.
With care she placed the vase behind his coat
still hanging on its hook beneath the stairs;
sensed a presence
that knew nothing of corruption.

28

FLIPHOP

The world is full of single flipflops,
their toeposts valiantly keeping strap and sole together
as they face a solitary future.

Some litter the tideline,
washed from helpless partners by capricious waves
while their owners paddled.

Others languish in laybys,
kicked out of cars that carry their other half
far into an uncertain future.

Some are abandoned in a weird rite of celebration
when young wearers decide
there is more fun in hopping;

while others are banished for losing their grip,
pairs wrenched wilfully apart,
one hurled this way, one that.

All share a common purpose,
determined to loaf around in hope
that fate will re-unite them with their mirror image.

The odds are not good.

CHRISTMAS CINQUAINS

Listen
where *White Christmas*
warns the countdown's begun.
Buy cards, buy gifts, wrapping paper -
just buy.

Pine scent
resins the air.
Fix baubles, wind tinsel,
embrace the boughs with coloured lights
and stars.

Kindle
the childhood joy
of visiting Santa,
waiting for thud of reindeer hooves
above.

Candles
reflect in glass,
glint on burnished dishes
as turkey, pudding, fruit and wine
are served.

Recall
a frightened girl
sweating in a stable
bringing the world its Light for you,
for all.

MENWITH HILL

From this high moor
Yorkshire stretches to infinity
of stunted grass, crag and boulder,
tough sheep you wouldn't argue with,
tumbledown stone shelters.

Heathcliff smoulders round every corner.
Cathy's ghost wails on the wind.
Hail-heavy clouds skulk,
blot out the blue.
Here is depth and space,
air so fresh it scours your lungs.

And at the peak of this rugged glory,
eight stark turbines winnow the wind,
harvest power, their shafts and spikes
a scar, an affront;
but let them whirr their way
into the country's heart -

they are the earth's great hope.

APPLE

I have no memory of growth on bough,
nor rendering from seam-locked nugget.
I was forged, a plaything for the gods,
beguiled into existence. Yet deep,
beneath my molecules, beneath my atoms,
instinct lingers.

I understand the yielding
of soft flakes of fruit beneath firm skin,
remembar pain's shock
when Eris etched *kallisti*
in my gold gleaming carapace. I sense
at my centre an essence of woman,
image of her parts; but know
I have no woman warmth, offer no comfort.

I am clash and discord, beauty's prize,
rich bauble, bringer of war.
Touch me cautiously.
I'll burn your fingers.

SNAPSHOTS OF MUM

She dressed me in pale blue tulle,
pink roses, for the beauty pageant
she didn't want me to enter:
called the judge an idiot when I didn't win.

She took me to collect
pussy willows, fill jars with tadpoles,
and never spilt a drop of pond water
as we cycled home.

She turned our table upside down,
a pirate boat for riding seven seas
instead of doing homework; made a shop,
a take-away, a post office, after school.

She could tidy the house
before we all got up, seat us
at a table gleaming blue and white with china,
groaning under eggs and buttered toast.

She bought me real pink nail varnish,
when all my friends had clear;
but couldn't quite cope
with the first shop for bras.

She knew the need
for raspberry milkshakes on a hot day;
produced sweets and snacks
from a bottomless handbag.

She was my Wonderwoman,
a hug in the cold, a project inspirer,
tear wiper, grandchild adorer;
and I wish I could tell her how I loved her.

CONFESSION

Finding I could not swallow pills,
couldn't aim a gun to take my life,
and throwing myself onto a sword
required a sense of direction,
I decided to eat myself to death.

I started small - a second cake,
extra fries, heavy on the mayo,
learned to choose a latte
instead of black coffee.

I progressed to handfuls of chocolate bars,
crackers and crisps, potatoes
slippery yellow with melted butter.

Soon I was only choosing *Eat All You Can* diners,
filling plate on plate, bowl on bowl,
scaling the heights of triple-decker ices,
cramming the span between coffee mug and lunch
with a club sandwich that could feed a family.

All this took time. I found a second job
moonlighting in an all-night deli,
needed extra cash to feed my resolve;
but before I had eaten myself to death
I found such unaccustomed ecstasy
in cream-filled gateaux
that I changed my mind.

Now I roll down the street, make chairs groan,
crush my puny mattress, leave bathtubs trembling …
but I'm happy
    happy
        HAPPY!

CONSIDERING *IF*

It lacks authority of *no*, demand of *me* -
but *if*'s two letters span
infinite possibility. They hover
over choices, clutch *only*
for the bleakest phrase, deride after *as*.

Embedded in difficulties,
urging toward cliff's edge,
if is the movement of drift,
nestles at the heart of life.

If pounds through the brain
before the dice of diagnosis land,
stays hands that fumble
heavy envelopes. *If* keeps you waiting,
allows you to delay.

A niggle to decisions,
gift for writers,
if encourages looking prior to leaps,
animates ideas of consequence.

It is your mother's warning,
impulse checker, parallel universe definer;

but what if … ?

SOMETHING IN THE DARK

I never knew this room was here,
thought this was a wall and not a door -
but something in the dark
drew my hand to the handle.

I am too naked to be vulnerable,
empowered by black oak
propelled to the table's head.

My fingers fix on carved lions
smoothed by centuries of handling, polishing.
I can feel the throaty rasp
of their purr.

I glide around the table,
bare feet soundless - enter
a shaft of moonlight
which smears my body silver.
That is when I realise
I am not alone.

The first rustle stirs shivers through my veins,
compounds with nameless footsteps
treading heavy measures, milling, crowding.
Now I can feel cold air on my face,
sense tiny hairs rising on my arms,
smell the musk of sweat.

Now I know what I must do -
force my way through thickened air
where phantom or memory crush,
lunge for the door.

There is no handle, no hinge,
no panels swing free to let me pass
back to my familiar corridors,
my staircase, the safe
of quilted sleep.

I look down, see nothing -
no body, no feet, no moonlight -
find myself dissolving
in the nowhere black.

SYNCHRONICITY

Love may be miraculous;
but the greatest miracle
is timing. For the earth was formed,
continents shifted, oceans learned tides,
glaciers crept, mountains soared,
valleys were etched; creatures left the sea,
became apes, became man.
And somewhere, somehow
it was arranged
that in one of those unfathomable
billions of moments
we two should be
in the same place
at the same time,
and fall in love.

HAMLET'S PSYCHOTHERAPIST DELIVERS HIS REPORT

I have made intensive study
  of this rather anxious prince,
and the levels of complexity
  would make a strong man wince.

He talks of hearing voices
  and he says he's seen a ghost
(with one ear that's full of poison)
  at the observation post.

His feelings for his mother
  are quite Oedipal, and yet
just the mention of his uncle
  makes him roll his eyes and sweat.

He's somewhat existentialist
  and queries if to be
or not is more acceptable,
  and then to what degree.

He wants his solid flesh to melt,
  and therefore he might seem
obsessed with his obesity
  and lacking self esteem.

He's into necrophilia
  and has been seen to mull
with over-zealous interest
  on poor Yorick's fleshless skull.

He's rather too hot-headed
  dealing with score-settling matters.

One violent, knife-led outburst
  left Polonius in tatters.

He needs a girl to show him love,
  set his libido free -
but the only one around here
  is as addle-brained as he.

So unless you want him sectioned
  in a mental institution,
then poison or a sword or both
  would be the best solution.

ARBOR LOW THOUGHTS

How many men have stood upon this place
and wondered by whose hand - when - why the stones
were bedded deep in grass? How many days
of quiet contemplation, undertones
of prayer, still whisper echoes on the breeze?
In sunlight, trippers walk their dogs, exclaim
at stone wall lattices, thick wads of fields,
or pace the moat. As dusk falls the terrain
disturbs with shapeless shadows, magnifies
a murmured lowing. New moon consecrates
the farmland with her silver; waxes, dies -
repeats again, again. The cold henge waits,
an undeciphered symbol from the past,
its secrets fading as the years fly fast.

GRANDMA

was not afraid to get her hands dirty,
cleaned in T. J. Hughes for decades,
cleaned (in her spare time) in Rodney Street
to eke out Grandad's warehouse wage.

When two sons had diphtheria
she walked miles to the hospital each day,
threw sweets up to the open window;
hoped four hands would still be there to catch.

Saturdays she toiled her shopping up Sleeper's Hill,
washed salad for the teatime ritual
when all the family converged, chatted,
bickered, shared specs to read the *Echo*.

Relaxing was a boxing match on telly -
roaring with the crowd, predicting victory
by who was wearing the biggest gloves -
or armchair wrestling along with Giant Haystacks.

She knew the good in neighbours,
never forgave the whole German race
for taking her eldest boy, always felt safe
when Anfield disgorged past her door.

At eighty-plus she joined the Over-Sixties,
escorted home those 'poor old souls'
a decade her junior. She'd have been here yet
if cancer hadn't worn the bigger gloves.

SPARK

It's a tingle that excites you,
  it's a whisper on the air,
it's the touch upon your shoulder
  when you know there's no one there.

It's the fraction of a second
  just before you find the word,
it's the perfume of forget-me-nots,
  a song you've never heard.

It's a half-remembered promise,
  it's a half-forgotten dream,
it's the crash of storm-tossed ocean,
  it's the ripple in a stream.

It's the echoing of silence,
  it's the dizzy spark that spins
when the crafting of a poem ends,
  and when the art begins.

NIGHT WALKER

Bats flitter, lifted on wind's screech,
fill twilight with spread black,
claws grasping the thickness of air.

He will walk tonight, snatch late magpies,
bite and gorge, skin rat and rabbit, learn
intensity of bone crunch, blood spurt.

He will watch where boys in hoodies,
long-limbed girls, tease and argue,
imagining his bony hands at throat or thigh.

He will chill autumn air with his presence,
swirl grey moths from his cloak,
disturb the dark with nightmares.

And when he is sated, he will fold himself
into swathing indigo, swoop and sweep
at one with bat and bruise and blackness.

STAGE MANAGEMENT

Nobody saw me sitting there, as row after row dispersed
to journey home, or after-show supper.
Someone turned off last lights, thudded the door,
and I ghosted the circle, sickly green
beneath emergency exit signs. I settled

further back into the scarlet plush of my seat;
heard through its threads last echoes of applause
fading at the final curtain, heard a swish
of skirt or sword, rustle of scripts, urgent calls to stage.

Nobody knew my silent drift to wings,
my hand on the cord shifting the tabs,
my fingers running over ranks of props.
I could walk freely, invade dressing rooms,
and, my eyes by now used to the gloom,
tweak costumes on their hangers,
wipe a slick of pancake from the shelf.

Nobody watched me climb,
higher and bolder, to gantries
where fresnels poised to cast their focussed pools,
or saw me swing back down ladder and rope.

Nobody guessed I paced the set,
angled a vase, straightened a chair.
My form imprinted itself
on the chaise longue; my feet
were the ones that shuffled the rug,
my breath that misted the glass.

Before early sun displaced shadows
I left, slipping between words' music and the morning,
edging from the real world into its shadow.
And nobody saw me go.

CATLANZA

Leaving the jetty is a slow glide,
smoothing through calmed wavelets.
Slip your shoes and slide barefoot
to the nets, sangria or a beer in hand.
Stretch out, and feel the tongue of sun
lick lazy warmth along your skin.

A moment - then you feel a surge
of engines lifting you to force through waves,
hypnotic rise and fall, and breezes
swirling heat away. Your head is filled
with bubbles frothing through your drink,
with laughter, with exhilaration.

The throbbing slows. A great white sail
unrolls, flaps, billows. Gulls circle,
anticipate butter chunks flung from a knife,
bread and scraps.

And now, at last, the steps are lowered
and you drop into the ice of ocean,
shiver, swim fast before cramp grips.
You float above rocks, above fish,
let breakers carry you, or ride them.

They call you back on board
for pasta, tuna, bread and salad.
Afternoon brings jet skis
bouncing from crest to crest,
zooming, spinning, and you praying
you'll be back safe; not wanting
the ride to end.

Your route to harbour
is more sedate, sun lower, sea calmer.
The luckless watch for dolphins
finds reward in a shoal of flying fish,
a quicksilver race with your craft.

Routine of drying, dressing, disembarking,
tips and final cups of wine
bridges you back to real life.
You are bussed to town,
hair matted, skin prickling,
to showers and choosing restaurants,
memories focussed on salt.

POSSESSED

I was amazed, astounded when I saw
that rat become a footman, six white mice
turned horses, when a coach stood at the door
in place of pumpkin. Jewels without price
gleamed at my throat, my rags became a dress
of purest silk, and there upon my feet
glass slippers, starred with crystal sparks, fluoresced.
I heard my Fairy Godmother entreat
that I should leave by midnight; but those shoes
kept dancing, waltzed my toes to spin with his,
whirled me around till I began to lose
all reason; head grew dizzy, senses fizzed.
    And now, enchanted, those glass slippers still
    possess me, twist my movement to their will.

END OF SEASON

In the nurse-busy rush
of tending, tidying, keeping your house
as you would once,
your garden was forgotten.

Today I trod
the too-green mossy clumps around your lawn,
saw heather's unruly spread
swamping more delicate flowers,
sensed late frost crumbling soil to clay.
Snowdrops dipped small heads
in lamentation; laurel drooped,
defeated; stripped hedges bristled.

I saw you sitting on the patio,
a cup of tea in hand, laughing
with sheer joy that we were all together;
recalled your pride in planting,
watering, nurturing. Now

you lie, your slight frame
scarcely moulding movement in the sheets,
need help to reach the bathroom,
help to eat, help
to turn over.

A late leaf that resisted autumn
looses its grip; spirals, dry, to soil,
a shadow to be trampled back to earth.

Your final countdown shudders.
Every grass blade holds its breath.

AFTERMATH

My mistress seems distracted, gives commands
that make no sense. She cries of blood. All day
she paces back and forth and wrings her hands.

It all began that time the king, his bands
of followers, attendants came to stay.
My mistress seems distracted, gives commands

then contradicts them, makes absurd demands.
She talks of witches' promises. The way
she paces back and forth and wrings her hands

makes doctors, servants, all her household brand
her wild, insane; but no-one will betray
their mistress. She, distracted, gives commands

and each of us pretends to understand
her garbled talk of letters, Duncan slain.
She paces back and forth and wrings her hands.

The thane has gone. His titles, castle, lands
mean nothing now; and, too disturbed to pray,
my mistress is distracted, gives commands.
She paces back and forth and wrings her hands.

ROLE MODEL

I have no great ambition;
all I want is a job I can do in my sleep,
enough pay to keep me, but not enough to worry me.

I want to spend my Saturdays
relaxed, mellow in yellow, TV rooted,
a can of beer, potato chips and do-nuts at my side.

I want a family who will look up to me,
a boy with spirit, a girl with brains
and, perhaps, a baby.

I want neighbours who'll lend me their lawnmower,
a bar where I am known by name,
convenience store with real convenience.

My classics teacher told me
I could learn a lot by studying Homer.
He was right.

WHEN DID YOU LAST SEE YOUR FATHER?

How must it have been for him,
that small boy, questioned by such ranks
of stern-faced men? How brave was he
to stand alone, no nurse or mother near,
anxious they'd hear his heart thudding?

He knew right and wrong,
but in that instant learned the need
for compromise. Total truth,
bible strong, could kill the man
who reared him, loved him. used to play with him
before those bleak-eyed soldiers came.

He was shrewd for his age, he knew
hesitation equalled guilt; but could he still
that memory-flash of safe places - his warm bed,
hot broth on winter evenings, throwing sticks
for his dog? Did inrush of the ordinary
steady his nerve, steady his voice?

His answer must have come,
a choice of words that would change
his life. Did he run from that room,
throw himself into his mother's arms,
sob with relief or pain?

I stand before the scene,
mother-long to hold him in my arms,
melt him into my bosom, hug him tight.
I want to see him run and laugh,
reclaim childhood -
but far more
I want to know his father came safe home.

DEATH MOUNTAIN

Everest grips its dead, anchors
husks of those who never reached the top,
who fell when sickness gnawed racked bodies,
desiccated.

You say it's hard to leave a corpse,
and struggle - snow blind, mind blind - to the summit;
harder still to leave
a nearly corpse, its lungs snatching
at thinning air, to close your ears
on last frail gasps.

How can it feel to meet again
those statue people, fixed along the route
when you descend? You know them by their clothes
but also read their faces,
recognise contortions of pain;
you need not fear decay, for weather's blast preserves.

Do you speak to them?

Safe down, safe home,
you tell of friends
who loved the climb so much
you chose to let them rest where they dropped -
say nothing of practicalities,
how nobody could shoulder
their dead weight,
carry it home.

Only in visions
do those bleak, iced faces loom,
murmur frustration at a task unfinished,

whisper their undead mantras
into the wailing winds.

ON THE BRINK

Our street was one-sided - every house was odd
for where the even houses should have been
parallel lines of road on road stretched forever
to the fairyland of cake shops, bus stops, playground.
Our corner shop had fresh-sliced bacon, tea, canned peaches,
jars pink with spearmint, primrose with sherbet lemons.
At three I stood on the counter, danced and sang,
was rewarded with chocolate. Flagged pavements
throbbed with dog-walkers, stop-for-a-gossipers,
ice-cream-van-chasers, back-to-school-foot-draggers.

On the cusp between war and swinging sixties
we knew we were on the brink ... though no-one guessed why.
In the next street, the street after, the street after,
Adrian Henri was picking up a paintbrush,
Roger McGough was picking up a biro,
Paul McCartney was picking up a guitar;
and just beyond the streets after that
the swelling Mersey shifted, surged, prepared
to shift the rhythm of the world forever.

MERRY CHRISTMAS

It's here again, the greeting
from all at No. 47. The postmark admits Yorkshire;
handwriting gives nothing away.
Mice in Santa hats cavort
around Christmas pudding crumbs -
so there's a sense of fun at 47.

I admire their tenacity,
writing year on year without acknowledgement.
I see them, practical, capable,
stringing garlands, hanging baubles,
inscribing their catch-all message
as they remember neighbours, nephews, friends.

And I am moved to wonder
which of *my* cards falls on fallow ground -
who's moved, meandered, died and never told us?
Who sees us like these folk from 47?
Who deciphers our scribbled names and says,
I don't know this lot. Friends of yours?

Yet something makes us send
these annually unrequited greetings
zinging through frosty streets,
as if we cannot bring ourselves to drop
a name once known, address
that might be misremembered.

I place the mice mid-mantelpiece
in proud celebration of those wishes
freely offered to one, and one, and all.
Thank you, 47 dwellers.
Merry Christmas.

WINTER SPORTS

A new light woke us,
unnaturally blue-white;
we drew bedroom curtains
on a Christmas-card scene. Trees
sagged under their burden of packed flakes,
roofs mimicked mountains,
a ski-run for robins. A church,
spread with a huge bleached shawl of snow,
glimmered in pale sun.

And in that dawn,
the only ones awake, the garden hidden,
in one mad moment
you dared me to strip,
race outside, lie naked in snow's sparkle
moulding angel forms. We lay
and laughed until the frost bit our flesh.

An hour later,
hot-showered and breakfasted,
we dressed in modest layers -
woolly coats, hats, gloves;
braved iced winds, plodded
embarrassed
down the path,
and with our boots
scuffed angels into anonymity.

Sometimes it's good
to kick over the traces.

IN THE GRAIN

Sapling days are never forgotten.
You keep an imprint of that first feel
of roots extending into earth, of sun
warming a green wisp that will become a trunk.

You never lose the memory
of seasons' passage, annual resurrection,
and growing in strength and sturdiness,
branches extending their supplication.

Even the shock and pain of felling
have their place in memory; for with them comes
anticipation of the moving on, turning beautiful
beneath a carpenter's hands.

But oh, if only I could shed
remembrance of being hacked
into crude spars, formed into a cross
dragged through streets, out of town, to a hilltop.

If only I could forget
the nails whose taint of blood and nerve
scarred my grain; dead weight
of the world's woe.

EXPLANATION

Do you remember, love, the day you swore
you couldn't live without me? Well,
it may please you to learn you won't have to.
Could you feel that breeze that ruffled your hair
though the air was still? That was my breath.
And the itch on your back you could not quite reach
was a stirring of my hand. Yes,
it was my voice that whispered your name
in the night, in your terrors. Yes,
I was the one who reached icy fingers
to shudder your spine.

And remember, love, when you go to her
and betray me by making those same empty promises,
I will be there to disturb your soft silences,
I will be watching and waiting,
a shadow to heighten your fears,
a clammy hand on your naked shoulder,
a cry in the stillness to unsettle your soul.

And remember, love, when you too yield
to the reaper's cold scythe, that I'll still be waiting.
And you will have to explain.

BIRD

The cat deposits a bedraggled mass
before me on the carpet,
smug smiles his expectation
of praise which doesn't come.

I watch his prey morph
into feathers, wings and tail,
a head, a tiny beak - and know
the coup-de-grace
must be my disgrace.

Before I can deliver it,
the transformation takes another twist
and black bead eye checks
the absence of grass or twig,
mouth V's open, delivers a *cheep*
too big for the body.

I lift him, marvel
that I feel no weight,
only a dust of down
and two long tail feathers.

Outside I place him
on pin-thin legs beneath
a hiding of leaves.
I watch for twenty minutes
from the window,
where sight or hint of me will not disturb.

He needs to re-learn safety
away from cat's mouth, human hand,
and is so still I think his heart has stopped.

Then with a wobbling rush
he turns to air, to light,
spreads perfect wings,
becomes himself.

And I laugh to see
his love of life so strong
it turns a feathered scribble to feisty flier.
And, warily at first,
I stretch *my* wings and look for flight.

DREAMS

I used to dream this day would come -
work over, nothing left to do but be -
and how we would travel the world together.

I dreamed of flying into Paris for lunch at Maxim's,
cruising the Nile to Abu Simbel's great temple,
trekking to Atahualpa's stronghold,
helicopters over the Great Barrier Reef.

I dreamed of driving Route 66,
balloon trips high above the Taj Mahal,
a gondola ride while the sun sets on St. Mark's Square,
bob-sleighing the Cresta Run.

So now we're here. It's happened;
and all I want to do is spend every hour, every day
holding your hand, gazing into your eyes.

Anywhere.

DNA

My science teacher tells me
we are closely related to the orang-utan,
both species sharing the ability
to solve problems with thought,
to express joy and sadness, to grieve.
Our DNA is different
by just three per cent.

I look at his red hair,
long arms, shambling walk;
and wonder whether, in some cases,
the difference might be two per cent.

INSIDE OUT

Feeling claustrophobic, a pair of lungs
decided to take the air;
so while their host lay sleeping
they loosed their moorings
and glided outside, waking the liver in passing.

Something's up, the liver thought,
stretching its lobes in unaccustomed space;
then not being one to miss an opportunity
it squelched its way downstairs
and headed for the bar.

Ruminating on all this, the stomach
flabbed its way through
and headed for the larder,
pleased to get away
from heart's monotonous thump.

Wait for us squawked the kidneys,
insisting on passing water
before they passed out,
shrugging themselves free of vein and tubule.

Digesting the situation, twenty feet of intestine
uncoiled, flung their length through the window
and snaked in the grass,
leaving the spleen
to mutter crossly to itself.

But as sun shooed the shadows away,
out-of-breath lungs regretted being so impetuous,
the liver and stomach reeled home
with kidneys in tow
and an early bird pecked at the lawn.

Slipping back was seamless, although
remaining organs glared their reproof.
Bladder prompted, their host stirred,
stretched and scratched,
surprised to recall an out-of-body experience.

OBSERVATION EXERCISE

Pretend this is your final week:
relish the taste of Monday, its too-fresh laundry-scented
sheets of wind. Listen where bees hum in buttercups.
Let every sip of Tuesday's coffee
swirl around your mouth, and feel its hot swallow
passing down your gullet. Explore the texture
of a peach, its peel, flesh and juice.
Pause on Wednesday's route to work
to hear grass growing in the park,
watch irises emerge from their scabbards,
unfurl their purple and gold.
When you meet a friend on Thursday,
treasure every word she speaks. Hoard them
to be inspected later as a child
examines pebbles salvaged from the shore.
Find your self on Friday. Feel
how your heartbeat reverberates around your body,
how your toes angle into your tread,
how your tongue lies in your mouth.
On Saturday stay in your house. Pick up
the nonsense objects you have acquired,
remembering each one's story. Then stroke sleek lines
of table, cupboard, drawers.
Go outside on Sunday. Lie on cold slabs of stone
to watch how clouds calculate the sky,
form into collages of nothingness, regroup. See
the incredible of blue and voice its shades -
azure, cerulean, aquamarine, duck-egg, cornflower.
Now leap to your feet, move forward
to the new week's promise.
Never shut your eyes.

A GIFT OF WATER

When lamp posts were sky tall
I looked up at those countless rows
of windows, and waved.
'Can you see her? Mummy's waving back'
was all the reassurance I needed. High above,
the sea-gazing Liver bird winked.

Pigeons came next, a monochrome flurry
that fluttered, settled, squabbled
over crumbs from jam sandwich crusts,
or dared to scrabble scratches on my hand.

Then the best treat; we tripped
down the floating pontoon
across slanting wooden slats,
and boarded the world's biggest boat.

Our Mersey ferry chugged its narrow path,
lifted and eased by light waves,
rocked me to the moment where sleep began …
and then a gentle bump nudged me awake.

'Over the Water' kept its mystique,
rose and fell as the ferry emptied, filled
while Nana and I giggled in the top-deck breeze,
shook salt onto crisps from blue paper twists,
picnicked on lemonade and custard creams.

Those Pier Head days of tram and gangplank
kickstarted a lifelong love of water,
an urge to watch tide's shifts,
to cruise, to swim, to know
keen smell of salt, the joy of bask and plunge.

A YEAR'S FULL CIRCLE

New Year: corks burst from their prisons;
kisses drown in froth. The telephone
defines geographies of love.

Epiphany: a space
the shape of a Christmas tree
absorbs songs and laughter, reflects grey light.

St. Valentine's Day: town is bleeding
with scarlet hearts. Roses and teddy bears
scream *Buy me!*

Easter: hope curls wetly
in a fragile shell.
Touch it with care.

Summer Holidays: I hold your hand
as we roar down the runway,
count two thousand miles of cloud.

Flower Show: onion pyramids,
cottage gardens, cup cakes, honey
jostle for prizes, sulk in second place.

August Bank Holiday: the last weekend
is lost in chianti. Daylight shrinks
into pinched evening.

Hallowe'en: trick or treat
slicks gaudy gloss, hints
at hidden menace.

Advent: tired days,
pregnant with promises,
stretch where a new light glimmers.

Christmas: joy oozes
from ribboned packages,
teaches a little more of love.

CANDLESTICKS

Two candlesticks in burnished ebony
adorned the mantelshelf, one at each side.
'The only gift your Grandad chose for me,'
my grandmother declared with gentle pride,
'the one surprise I didn't have to pick.'
She touched each barley-sugar-twisted stem
as if caressing porcelain. Her quick
seamstress's fingers stroked and polished them.
No candle ever burned there, no wax dripped,
no smoky wick smeared charcoal on the wood.
When Grandad died, her tearful glances slipped
to fix on them, as if they understood.
  Years on, those candlesticks are mine, stand fast -
  a talisman of contact with my past.

NOT FAR FROM HAMELIN ...

Vast and reaching, this mountain stands
lush on its lower slopes, edged
with trees and grass. Above
a sparser scrub mottles rock.
Only chattering of sparrows moves the air.

But stay until moonrise jostles evening
to see rook's grey turn purple,
bruised and ominous, shrub scarred;
to watch leaves twist and writhe,
trunks thicken with threat.

Listen past the quiet
after birds have flown. A new strain
starts its murmur, crescendoes
into lament, becomes a wail -
near human, wholly agony.

Decay's sickly pall seeps from the ground,
spreads its stained blanket over grass.
Air chills until it hurts to breathe,
freezes gasps of fear, fixes feet
to earth, so there is no escape.

Minutes teeter; hours crawl
until dawn's first sliver
frees the grip
of mountain's menace, mocks
as early warmth tingles grass blades.

But if you would evade the mountain's hold,
ignore tales of a man of music
and his retinue of dancing children.

Close your mind to legends of rock
splitting in welcome, sealing sons and daughters inside.

STARGAZING

A galaxy clusters beneath my slow drift
sloe-shadowed, forming constellations
where random stars make patterns -
plough and swan, Orion, Cassiopeia.

Clumsy with fins and wetsuit, I heave air,
see motion through mask's distortion,
watch asteroidea mimic orbits
among scattering of shells, nebulae of crabs.

For thirty pressured minutes I circle
in my pre-birth element, learn my elliptic, sound
my place between space-blue and seabed's rocks.

Beached, I plod to meet
my sons, intent on digging sand,
building castles crumbling before paper flags blow.
Their father waits and watches, smiling lazy.

And I, who have seen in one half hour
reflections shifting shoals of ocean's treasure -
bloodless, brainless, near-blind -

I cannot look with love on ordinary life,
am overwhelmed by water. I long to split,
divide into tentacles to clone another me, another,
till I can fathom infinity of stars.

HELL HATH NO FURY

He thinks that I've capitulated; joke!
When Moth and Cobweb told me what he'd done -
bewitching me, queen of the fairy world,
with drops of love-in-idleness - I knew
that I could work it to my own advantage.
He made a fool of me, I'll not deny,
but he won't do it twice. For I'm resolved
to learn those skills that mortal women have,
to flirt and tease, cajole and flatter, charm
until he is besotted. Then I'll turn
my back, ignore his wheedling kisses, mock
his efforts to make love to me, and laugh
his macho image into scorn. He thinks
it sport to pair me with a braying ass,
a yokel weaver? Well, we'll see who laughs
the last and longest. One thing I have learned:
the bedchamber can make such fools of men,
and he's no better than mere mortals. I'll
inflame his want until he's sick with lust,
and begging for my favours. Then I'll seize
my darling changeling boy, escape with him
into the forest's welcoming embrace;
and from a distance watch him, curse him, tell
his dalliance with that horse-faced Amazon
to all the subjects of his fairy kingdom.
And when he's on his knees I'll make my move,
return in triumph, take my rightful place
upon his throne - and watch him hit rock bottom.

SEIZE THE DAY

I shall make this day my lover,
stroke its coral dawn into wakefulness,
murmur sweet endearments
while squirrel and skylark
take place of fox and owl.
I shall caress the warm wind
that teases cherry blossom's froth,
and the swish of water busy in reeds.
I shall hold the bustle and noise
of a glad-to-be-alive town,
bleat of new lambs on remote hillsides,
hope of every seed that locks to earth.
When afternoon subsides into lengthening shadows,
I shall run my fingers down the spine of evening,
blow kisses to each constellation.
And at the close of day
I'll wrap my arms around its promise of tomorrow,
knowing this love
will never let me down.